The pineapple is the king of fruits and is given as a symbol of welcome throughout the tropics ...

... other forms of hospitality are equally welcome

India Hicks and David Flint Wood

ISLAND LIFE Inspirational interiors

Foreword by Ralph Lauren   Photography David Loftus

Stewart, Tabori & Chang

New York

For my eccentric and beautiful sister Edwina,
through whom I met David   IH

For Felix, Amory and Conrad   DFW

*The authors will be donating a percentage of
their royalties to Dunmore School on Harbour Island*

Published in 2003 by
Stewart, Tabori & Chang
An imprint of Harry N. Abrams, Inc.

First published in Great Britain in 2003 by
PAVILION BOOKS

An imprint of Chrysalis Books Group plc

The Chrysalis Building
Bramley Road, London W10 6SP

Library of Congress Cataloging-in-Publication Data

Hicks, India.
    Island Life : inspirational interiors / India Hicks and David Flint Wood ; foreword by
  Ralph Lauren ; photography by David Loftus.
        p.cm.
      ISBN-13: 978-1-58479-317-5
      ISBN-10: 1-58479-317-1
  1. Hicks, India—Themes, motives. 2. Interior decoration—Bahamas—History—20th
century—Themes, motives. I. Wood, David Flint. II. Title
    NK2047.6.H53A4 2003
    747'.097296—dc21

                                                            2003052983

The text of this book was composed in Joanna MT
Designer: Paul Welti
Commissioning editor: Kate Oldfield
Project manager: Claire Wedderburn-Maxwell
Copy editor: Alison Wormleighton

Printed in Singapore.

10 9 8 7 6 5 4

HNA ▪▪▪▪▪
harry n. abrams, inc.
a subsidiary of La Martinière Groupe
115 West 18th Street
New York, NY 10011
www.hnabooks.com

Contents

I first came across India in 1989 and I think it's true to say that in her first photo shoot for a magazine she was modeling my clothes. The relationship continues to this day; India has continued to model for us and the Polo Ralph Lauren team have stayed at Hibiscus Hill, using the house as a location for ad campaigns.

As the granddaughter of one British icon (Lord Mountbatten of Burma, the last Viceroy of India) and the daughter of the late David Hicks (an icon of international design), I was not surprised that she would develop into more than, what they used to call, 'a great society beauty'.

The style of her homes on the island is impressive and I was also captivated by the romance of the story that lay behind their creation. It strikes me that many people may dream of leaving high-profile lives in New York or London to go and live on a tropical island, but very few actually do it — or have the imagination and creativity to make it work.

I have my own houses in the islands and I applaud the effort that must have gone into achieving what India and David have created.

The seductive combination presented in _Island Life_ — a combination of international lives, classic British good taste (including its eccentricities), and the traditions and flavour of the Caribbean — cannot fail to inspire anyone who has the good fortune to pick it up.

RALPH LAUREN, 2003

Introduction: This side of paradise

The history and climate of the Caribbean have dictated the style of the islands' homes.

A hurricane survivor stays doggedly upright in the shallows of the island.

The view from the harbour. If you took away the outboard motors this would be a scene that has hardly changed in the last two hundred years.

A typical cottage in the town. The architecture was brought down to the islands at the end of the 1700s by settlers from the eastern seaboard of the United States.

Inspired by the past

The idea of life on a tropical island appeals, in one form or another, to almost everybody. It certainly did to us, and it continues to do so to the extent that over a period of six years we have decorated, restored, or built three houses and a hotel on two islands in the West Indies.

Except for the last house featured in this book – which constitutes an act of love and respect for the genius of the late David Hicks, celebrating his own unique interpretation of island life – these buildings are products of our imaginations, hard work, and often heated debate. They have come to reflect a style most easily recognized as "plantation" or "colonial" but hopefully also include some original ideas and more than a little native wit (both our own and the local variety).

A great deal of our inspiration is drawn from the island we live on: its light and colours; its flora and fauna; local materials and craftspeople; and, last but by no means least, its history.

Much of the romance and drama of this history is captured in the novels and short stories about life on tropical islands, by writers such as Robert Louis Stevenson, Somerset Maugham, Joseph Conrad, and Graham Greene.

In between the fact and the fiction, they conjure up images of sepia–toned photographs of houses with wide verandahs, dark wooden floors, and ceiling fans, peopled by groups in white linen with straw hats, sipping cocktails. And they evoke the bustle and clutter of men unloading ships at the docks while women of every hue, in elaborate hats and headscarves, barter and gossip in colourful markets.

After the day's work is done on these islands, the homes people return to, whether they are "plantation

Pineapples were a source of prosperity to the island for many years. A traditional symbol of welcome, they have long been used by carpenters as a decorative motif. Skills other than carpentry were also passed on through the years – the faster schooners, for example, were used as blockade runners during the American Civil War, while their descendants did well rum-running during Prohibition in the 1920s.

houses" or cottages, reflect their owners' lives and the conditions in which they live.

In many of the foreigners' homes, nostalgic elements from the home country, along with furniture, pictures, and objects from travels, combine with influences from the new surroundings, reflecting their owners' willingness to assimilate and adapt.

The meeting of these cultures is reflected in both island life and island style. Indeed, these often disparate elements of decorating, juxtaposing old and new, are now often emulated, along with the colour schemes, in the world of interior design.

The island we live on was originally settled in the mid-1600s by people from New England and Bermuda seeking freedom of worship, who were literally washed up by shipwreck. In the early 1700s the population became what must have

been an interesting mix of fishermen, boat builders, smugglers, wreckers, and pirates (Captain Rackham and the two most famous women pirates, Anne Bonny and Mary Read, conducted their business here).

The town was properly laid out in the late 1700s, when an influx of Empire loyalists from the American colonies established the architectural style that prevails today: weatherboard cottages similar to those of New England and the Carolinas, along with stone-built town houses and grand plantation owners' homes. Sugar cane and pineapple plantations thrived for a while and with them the boat-building industry that produced the schooners and sloops, crowding the harbour before heading north to America. Many of these carpenters' skills, transferred to buildings on the land, are still evident today in the islands' homes.

Pineapple shapes are found everywhere on the island: on gateposts, carved from wood on rooftops, and on furniture. The simple charm of these cut-outs on a picket fence is inspiring.

Time and the elements

The major factor that influences island life is the weather. Few things last for ever or even very long in the tropical climate. Everything is under attack, as wind, sand, sun, salt, rain, and humidity all conspire to accelerate the process of decay.

Aside from the nightmare of having to conduct an almost continuous campaign of property maintenance, the patina of age that the elements lend is definitely part of the charm of the style. Anything made of wood, including furniture and floors, soon loses its sheen; fabrics fade, and colours and varnishes soften, so that a "lived in" atmosphere is almost unavoidable.

For pragmatists who like their home to look well used and as though it has lived a long and full life, the climate is an asset. In the same way that a black-and-white or sepia-toned photograph can lend nostalgia to a recent photograph, the elements here have a major impact on the houses, particularly their facades.

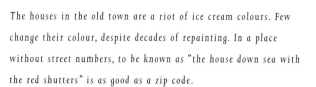

The houses in the old town are a riot of ice cream colours. Few change their colour, despite decades of repainting. In a place without street numbers, to be known as "the house down sea with the red shutters" is as good as a zip code.

Protection and decoration

Paint is extremely expensive, and so are the people who put it on, for applying it properly takes time. After the supply of indigenous hardwoods on the island was exhausted, the necessity for paint increased as it is first and foremost for protection. Even before that, colour had a practical function – it offered visible proof of the financial capacity to afford it.

(Left and above) *As churches and the sea have fed the souls and bodies of the islanders since the arrival of the earliest settlers, the similarity of the colours and shapes in these two pictures – taken within a hundred feet (30m) of each other – may not be purely coincidental. Then again, perhaps it's the priest's boat.*

Nature and design

The island has become a celebration of paint, and even as you approach by boat, one of the first things that you notice is the explosion of colour. If you come from a northern country or city, this is one of the enduring and joyous aspects of visiting or living here. Like many people before you, you could exhaust your powers of description and your box of watercolours in attempting to describe it.

(Opposite and above) Observing the recurrence of colours and shapes, coincidental or deliberate, in nature and design becomes irresistible. Here, pandanus leaves are mirrored by a green staircase against a yellow wall.

Repeating themes

You do not need to be a qualified architect in order to notice the common themes among the older houses of the island, or to appreciate how these have inspired the more successful recent buildings. The similarities range from fundamental characteristics of structure or layout, to intricate decorative details.

Building on a basic square with windows and doors on opposite sides allows a house to "breathe" whatever direction the prevailing breeze is coming from. For houses on high ground, this principle can virtually remove the need for modern air-conditioning. From the simplest "shotgun shack" (so called because if you fired a shotgun through the front door you would not hit a wall) to the grandest plantation house, the governing wisdom lies in cross-ventilation.

(Opposite and above)

The beauty of this "Sunday best" lace dress echoes the intricate fretwork and gate of a town house.

The decoration of homes always concerns not just shape and size, but also details – everything from paint colours on walls and on storm shutters to gardens that "frame" the house – plays its part. A Caribbean tradition, inherited particularly from French islands, is to decorate the outside of the house. Gingerbread-style carving, along with intricate patterns on fences and balustrades, adds to the joy of a stroll through this side of paradise.

What is safe to say is that most of the householders on the island are extremely "house-proud," possibly because of the kindred spirit that comes from knowing how much effort goes into maintaining property in this climate.

Introduction:
This side of
paradise

Inside out

It is characteristic of formerly English islands that most houses have porches or verandahs. These serve two main purposes, both a result of adapting to the climate. Primarily they allow sitting outside in the shade so as to catch all the available fresh air. Even when a verandah is not in use, the overhanging roof shades windows and doors to help keep the rooms cool. The other main purpose is protection against the rain. When it rains in the tropics, the water seldom falls vertically, as it is almost always carried by wind. Verandahs prevent water from coming through doors and windows, so that they do not necessarily have to be closed – a big advantage, since it can still be very hot even while it is raining.

With so much of life being conducted outdoors in this part of the world, verandahs are a perfect way to be half in and half out of the house. The best design is when the verandah "wraps around" the house, allowing you to follow the breeze and avoid the sun for the whole day. It also means that on particularly windy days you can find shelter on the lee side of the house.

In the town, there is another, undeclared benefit of verandahs – the opportunity to observe and over-hear passers-by without detection. (It's no surprise that people mumble, almost always speaking in whispers, and that no one uses names when gossiping.)

Introduction:
This side of
paradise

(This page and previous page) Porches and verandahs, a typical feature of British islands in the tropics, are cool, shaded areas that unite the house and garden.

Island life

It is important to remember, through all this celebration of smart, largely foreign-owned homes, that the vast majority of the island's population are direct descendants of African slaves, brought here by plantation owners in the 1700s.

With the slaves' emancipation in the mid-1800s and finally the island's independence from Britain in 1973, it is these locals (who proudly call themselves "natives") who have set the pace and tone of the islands. Their welcome and goodwill towards foreign residents and visitors allow the island to function.

Their history and its influences are felt daily in the life of this place. The music, which is ubiquitous, varies from the African rhythms of vast goat-skinned drums used in the "Junkanoo" carnival at Christmas (and often heard late into the night during the months of practice leading up to it) to the formality of seemingly weekly parades and marching bands, inherited from the British.

There is also plenty of dry humour and the natural tendency towards homespun philosophy that probably characterizes the people of small islands everywhere.

Dressing up and going out, whether it is to church or out dancing – and sometimes it is hard to tell which is which – is a popular pastime, as attested by the fact that there is always a celebration going on somewhere.

(Left) Young drummers being coached for the annual "Junkanoo" carnival –
introduced by African slaves centuries ago to celebrate Christmas and New Year.

(Overleaf) The horse-drawn carriage for sunset tours and weddings,
decked out in palm fronds and flowers.

Introduction:
This side of
paradise

When they first see this, a lot of tourists imagine that it is an obeah or voodoo shrine. In fact, it is "Ralph's aura corner," a wonderful collection of fortune-cookie-style philosophy and

humour painted on driftwood. It is the life's work of Uncle Ralph, a local house-painter.

The house on the hill

Hibiscus Hill was built in the 1950s, but we have endeavoured to make the villa look like it was built in the 1850s.

*The house on
the hill*

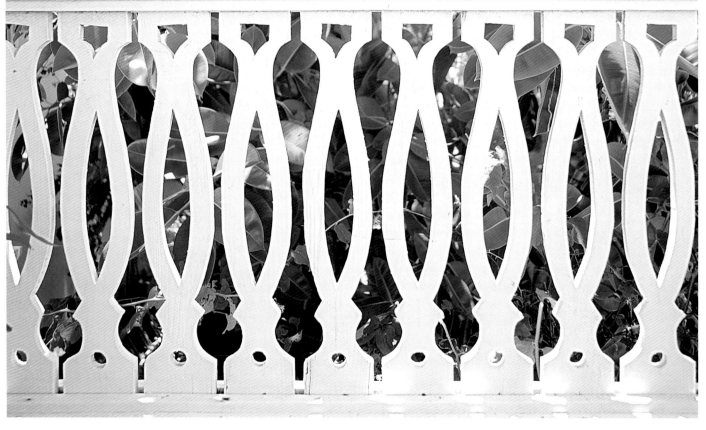

Inspired by older houses on the island, we designed a balustrade for the verandahs and had it cut out by hand (as is obvious on close inspection).

It helped "backdate" the house immediately.

Balustrades and boats

On this island, a sandbar in truth, which is only four miles (6.4km) long and a mile (1.6km) wide, Hibiscus Hill sits back from the ocean on high ground. Fortunately, this means that it does not bear the full brunt of the wind and salt, an important factor in living here all the year round.

The house sits in three acres (1.2ha) of rolling garden that stretches from the top of the dunes and is bordered by jungle on two sides with a valley of coconut palms on the other. With its own path to the beach and the

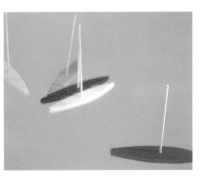

The offcuts from the balustrade automatically suggested themselves as boat-shaped, solving the problem of our son's first birthday present.

luxury of a swimming pool, it looks out over the distant rooftops of the town to the harbour and the setting sun.

Built in the 1950s and subsequently extended, the house has "good bones" and many of the important structural features of Caribbean style such as verandahs and a high, pitched roof. Inside are rooms with tray ceilings made of tongue-and-groove cypress. When we bought the house, overhead fans were already fitted, and many of the windows had plantation shutters to screen the sun.

The organic house

The inside of the house was the perfect "blank canvas" when we bought it. With its white cement-tiled floors, white and glass furniture, and white walls, it was completely practical. Onto this blank canvas we have projected our own colours, tastes, and styles, as one does to create a home that is permanently lived in and grows with the family.

Compromises have been negotiated and individual tastes accommodated, as personal collections of pictures, books, and furniture have arrived. While interior-designed houses can sometimes lack the feeling of being personally owned or lived in, this house has the stamp of its owners throughout.

When you have paintings and books, you can re-create your home anywhere, whether it is two city blocks or an ocean away, as these key elements always transfer familiarity. Everything else can be subject to the excitement of change – as it certainly was here.

In the first nine months the entire ground floor changed colour three times, and friends began to describe Hibiscus Hill as the "organic house." A very pale grey and white for the entrance hall, dining room, and sitting room were eventually settled on, as these colours are calming and peaceful (reasons that first attracted us to living on the island). Over the course of the next six years, an overall style evolved that is most easily described as colonial or plantation style.

The entrance to the house divides the dining and sitting rooms. Bleached shells, coral, and local straw-work establish fairly immediately that you're on the islands. Racks of family photographs line one wall of the dining room, a form of gallery that is easily updated.

Wood, paper, and straw

In place of the original cement, tile, and glass, the materials now used throughout the ground floor are softer and more natural. In the dining and sitting rooms the floors are now overlaid with wood, using unusually large fir planks that are a foot (30cm) wide and in some cases a full sixteen feet (5m) long. They have been stained a dark oak shade, but the climate, coupled with the daily sanding that they receive from children and dogs fresh from the beach, has given them an aged patina of their own.

Many of the hats over the archway have been bought at the local straw market by family and friends and then left in the house. Like the books, they have become a sort of library for subsequent visitors.

The Victorian dining table and chairs came from New Orleans. Travel is one of the most effective sources of inspiration, and New Orleans is perhaps the most urbane and sophisticated of sub-tropical cities. Trawling the antique and junk shops there yielded twenty-two packing cases of furniture and objects for the house. It is never a good idea to condense all your furniture buying into one afternoon, but living on an island reduces the opportunity to take time and care.

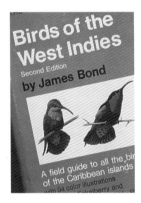

Not just books

The wall of the sitting room, punctuated by the archway to the dining room, has been lined with classically styled bookshelves, designed and built on site from inexpensive plywood and painted white. These shelves are more than a mere means of storing books, or even a family library, as they are used to exhibit objects from family history, travels, and simple "finds" on the island.

(*Above*) Birds of the West Indies *is the standard reference book on its subject and is found in most of the old houses here. It is said that Ian Fleming, while staying with a distant cousin of India's in Nassau, was looking for a name for the hero of his new spy novels, and found it on the cover of this book. (Below) The model of the J Class yacht helps to break up the vertical and horizontal lines of the books and shelves. (Overleaf) Binding the books in manila paper has created a warm-toned and uniform background for an eclectic assortment of objects.*

The books are themselves part of the decorating scheme, inspired by David Hicks's library in England, in which all of the books were rebound at vast expense in red leather. A spell of bad weather on the island, resulting from a long, drawn-out hurricane season, allowed a similar approach to be taken here (though without a similar budget) – all the hardback books were rebound in manila paper bought from the local hardware store.

The spines of the books create a sepia backdrop, reminiscent of the wood-shingled roofs found all over the island. They provide a framework for displaying particularly striking book covers, which are turned face-on, and an ever-changing series of unrelated but tonally consistent sculptural shapes. A large model of a sailing ship with canvas sails stands on top of the cabinets in front of the books.

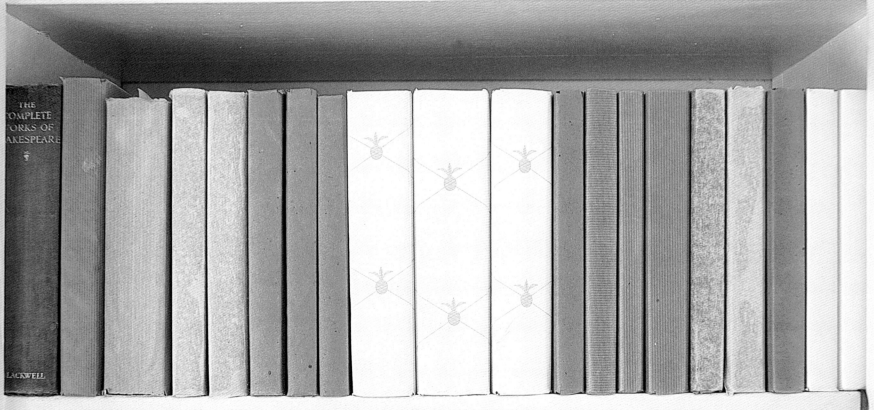

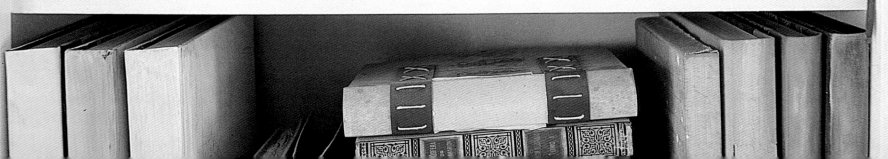

Rules are
made to be broken

From the glare of the sea and the vibrancy of the tropical flowers, to the kaleidoscopic tones of the houses and shutters in the village, the island is full of light and colour. For many people with houses here, the interiors provide an opportunity to celebrate all this colour, in rooms that go through the shade card from allamanda to aquamarine.

However, almost all the rooms in this house are decorated in the fairly muted, almost sepia tones of wood and in shades not too far from white, offering a respite from the brightness outside.

There is therefore no explanation for the use of a pink somewhere between bougainvillea and hibiscus on the staircase — other than that it's such a surprise that it makes people smile. The white paint of the mirror frame and the table reinforces the strength of the wall colour.

The sign that sits at the top of the stairs had been discarded, just as its advice had, next to the swimming pool when we bought the house.

The house on
the hill

Evergreen

Tropical flowers don't last long after they're cut. When Hamish Bowles came down to photograph our house for American *Vogue*, he went out and cut palm fronds for a large vase from North Africa that stands on the sitting room fireplace. Now the room looks "undressed" without them. Thankfully palm fronds last and are not in short supply here.

The house on
the hill

(Left and right)
*A series of naïve paintings
depicting the gathering of crops
including coffee, cotton, and
palm fronds.*

Local colour

One of the elements of decoration most difficult for any group of people to agree on is art. In the Caribbean, painting at its best is in a naïve style. The deceptively simple tropical paintings by the French artists Paul Gauguin and Henri Matisse are the most

successful examples of this style. As regards the more affordable paintings that can be found in the islands, the trick is to avoid those attempting sophistication.

Two studies in different styles

To build two studies for ourselves, the roof was taken off a storeroom and laundry, a storey was added, and the resulting space was divided in half by a wall with glass doors. Having two studies not only affords privacy but also provides the opportunity to decorate without compromise. The individual styles used in these two rooms are markedly different, yet going from one to the other is not too much of a visual shock.

(Opposite and above) Mahogany-stained bookshelves display wooden objects from all over the world: a vase and bowl that were turned on a nearby island; the ubiquitous obelisks, this time from North Africa; a two-hundred-year-old English painting box; and even a box containing a caviar set made in Kenya from ostrich eggs.

Model sailboats recur throughout the house. In many cases they seem to us to be sculptures in their own right. As well as fine craftsmanship, they offer a reminder of the time when islands were first explored and settled in what Joseph Conrad described as: "those unprotected days when we were content to hold in our hands our lives and our property."

The house on
the hill

Tablescapes

David Hicks was renowned for using almost any available flat surface to create what he termed "tablescapes": arrangements of objects old and new, often incorporating experimental combinations of colours and textures. This inheritance has become something of an obsession in this house.

In a lost war with a more minimalist style of decorating, tablescapes afford an opportunity to marshal large collections of objects regarded by a previous generation as "dust traps."

The centre of the sitting room is dominated by a large white table top which holds a type of "mini-museum" of disparate and somewhat eccentric objects collected over time. For example, antique watercolour and jewellery boxes, backgammon and domino sets, a pigskin writing case, and a wooden toy car are all held together by colour and shape. As a series of brown rectangles arranged in their own rectangular jigsaw, they create a unique conversation piece.

The pervasive influence of David Hicks in this house is nowhere more obvious than in the use of obelisks, a form he employed extensively in both his interiors and his designs for gardens.

A table next to the sofa in the sitting room holds a group of glass crystal obelisks found in London. Repeating the theme of transparency is a photograph framed between two sheets of glass. In front stands a Perspex (Plexiglas) box holding a group of fish carved from red coral. Although these elements are unrelated in content, the reflection and refraction of light from their surfaces tie them together.

(Above) The obelisk, positioned in a shaded corner of a terrace. The result is surprisingly effective for a first-time attempt at sculpture, but the process of construction was straight out of Laurel and Hardy. (Right) Slightly less monumental but no less striking, crystal obelisks are grouped on a table in the sitting room.

In a rash moment, we decided to build an eight foot (2.4m) tall obelisk. Having made the base, by pouring cement and rock into a two-foot (60cm) cube made of plywood and reversed crown moulding, the mason became slightly over-confident. The mould for the needle was set in place and then poured, whereupon the plywood burst and deposited half a ton of fast-drying cement on the terrace. We have since rather shied away from sculpture.

Perhaps not obvious in this picture,
these chairs are child-sized. When the
television is working, the boys sit there
with all the seriousness of movie
producers reviewing the day's "rushes."

In what is the rather more predictably masculine study, the atmosphere is something like the captain's cabin on an old schooner (possibly crossed with a junk shop).

Mahogany-stained bookshelves with window seats face each other from opposite walls. The flush door handles are brass ring handles bought from a boat chandler.

Books and objects from travels line the shelves, and the walls are covered with pictures from Haiti, Cuba, Europe, and America. The Indian desk holds a barely organized riot of photographs and scrapbooks as well as pots and cigar boxes containing rubber stamps, pens, and brushes.

Sitting here at night, with the windows open and no sound but the overhead fan and the surf on the beach, you can easily imagine yourself a character in some Joseph Conrad or Somerset Maugham story.

A row of ink bottles
from Switzerland and Italy, used for scrapbooks and
diaries, sketches and letters.

The house on
the hill

Night and Day

Because the sun is so strong in the tropics, it is an advantage to use a lot of dark wood and colours that absorb light. Artificial light is seldom necessary here in the daytime.

When night falls, to avoid feeling as though you are sitting in a "real" office, don't use overhead light – table lamps create a much softer effect.

Another alternative is recessed lighting, particularly lights that can be adjusted and specifically directed. To highlight tablescapes, pictures, and objects placed on bookshelves, this directional lighting can be particularly useful.

The subject of light has obsessed artists for centuries – and some, like Paul Gauguin and many of the Impressionists, felt compelled to travel to the tropics in an attempt to capture it.

But for those of us more likely to buy art than to create it, light, especially in this part of the world, can pose serious problems.

(Above) A wooden cast of a child's shoe and a carpenter's ruler from India sit next to quartz stones found on an African beach and a toy car bought in Rome.

(Right) An oil painting set has been left open to encourage its use.

The house on the hill

While the fading and softening effects of the sun can make fabrics and wood more attractive, these effects can be completely ruinous, in particular to pictures and books. It is important to establish where the sun falls on walls before placing anything that you value on them. Many rooms in the tropics are kept deliberately dark for just this reason.

In this consciously low-tech office, a pool of light from a wood and steel reading lamp illuminates an old-fashioned telephone on the desk. Next door, the "red" office is a different story – directional spotlighting enhances a clean, crisp, and altogether more businesslike space furnished with computers and a fax machine.

(Left) Scrapbooks and travel journals cover David's desktop.

(Opposite) Some of David's oil paintings (possibly proof that the man who is self-taught has been to the worst school in the world).

Seeing red

The red office is a true Hicks family affair. The local painters went to great lengths to explain that it was highly irregular to use gloss paint on "dry wall." However, they failed to appreciate that the fact that they'd never done it before was the crowning argument in its favour.

Four coats of what could be described as Chinese red later, the legacy of David Hicks's use of strong colour and unexpected textures had again proved its success.

Although one might expect this red to make the room seem like an inferno in the tropical heat, it in fact absorbs much of the light that pours through the windows and so seems "cool."

Originally all the trim in this study was dark stained, but painting it white has made it seem much fresher, and accentuated the room's symmetry. This is another example of strong contrasts being as – or more – effective than consciously choosing colours from the same palette. This might prove exhausting in every room in the house but works well as an unexpected "accent".

Family photographs surround a Swedish blown glass vase.

The paintings in the red office are, literally, heirlooms. Painted by David Hicks on a tour of Italy in the late 1950s, they are studies of architectural sites and scenes using vibrant blocks of colour such as mint and rose skies and crimson courtyards. Over these colours are the skeletons of the buildings in white.

(Above and left) The staircase leading up to the red office is hung with David Hicks's remarkable architectural paintings.

The striking contrasts of Chinese red and white along with the strength of these pictures create a powerful impact.

The pictures are inspiring as an exercise in creative, lateral thinking, and hanging them on these red walls guarantees that "going to the office" is not the regular commute.

In the interests of "keeping it in the family" we asked India's brother, Ashley Hicks, to design a pair of large cupboards that could hold all the stationery and files that accumulate, particularly since office supplies are bought in bulk while abroad.

Ashley did drawings while here on holiday and one of the local carpenters was able to make them in a couple of days so that the designer could see his finished ideas before he left for England.

The only technical difficulties arose from the quality of the mirror glass used for the door panels. This was so thin that every time somebody closed a door, a panel would shatter, with the risk of impromptu amputation. New mirrors came from Nassau, and now replenishing the fax paper no longer represents a health hazard.

The cupboards were designed by India's brother,
Ashley Hicks, using "snake" handles produced in India for
his furniture-design business.

The house on
the hill

And so to bed

The master bedroom, like the sitting room, has a "tray ceiling" so called because it appears like an inverted tea tray. Tray ceilings are typical of Caribbean homes, adding height that helps to accommodate ceiling fans and to keep the air circulating.

In both rooms the wood ceilings had been limed (pickled), which involves rubbing white paint first onto and then off the grain of the planks. This had left them a pinkish grey colour with the problem that in the afternoon the strong light would bounce around and turn the walls a strange shade of lilac.

The house on
the hill

*(Right and opposite)
We found our bed in a
magazine advertisement. It
was made by a furniture
company that named each of
the pieces in their line after
the viceroys of India. This
one was called the "Lord
Mountbatten Tester Bed."*

*(Opposite) These walls are
covered by hand-coloured,
tropical bird prints found
in London and dated 1820.
They reinforce the feeling
of a period plantation
house, created by the more
modern furniture.*

We painted the ceilings white in order to overcome the lilac effect but then found that the feeling of extra height that this produced made the room seem out of proportion. The solution was to buy a large and particularly tall four-poster bed.

ANTHONY
POWELL
• • •
A DANCE TO
THE MUSIC
OF TIME

ANTHONY
POWELL
• • •
A DANCE TO
THE MUSIC
OF TIME

ANTHONY
POWELL
• • •
A DANCE TO
THE MUSIC
OF TIME

ANTHONY
POWELL
• • •
A DANCE TO
THE MUSIC
OF TIME

MICHAEL ONDAATJE

ANITA SH

The bedside tables offer another opportunity to create tablescapes from prized objects, and they are continually subject to review. As well as supporting more predictable things like family photographs and night-time reading, they hold souvenirs of recent travels and more sentimental memorabilia. Fresh flowers are also often placed on the tables in small, unfussy vases. As well as the more valued objects, we get just as much pleasure from seeing a pretty watch lying on the table top, even if it has been broken for years.

(*Above*) *A watercolour Valentine by David is juxtaposed with vintage Masai beads bought in Nairobi. The yellow rose set in Perspex (Plexiglas) is from the wedding bouquet of Diana Princess of Wales and was given to India as one of her bridesmaids.*

(*Opposite*) *The shells capped in beaten silver are from the west coast of India, while the toy animals were made in Kenya from banana leaves twisted around wire. The enamel and silver alarm clock was designed by David Hicks just before his death.*

(*Left*) *A hand-drawn millennium greeting card framed between Perspex (Plexiglas) blocks sits alongside a picture of one of our sons, only a few weeks old, in the arms of a friend.*

Nights on the tiles

When we bought the house, the master bedroom had wall-to-wall carpet. Taking it up revealed that the original floor was made of tiles, manufactured by Cubans brought to Nassau in the 1950s to help in the construction of the British Colonial Hotel. We have great fun spotting the same tiles in the most obscure places all around the island, such as on the floor of the bar in one of the less salubrious night spots.

The room has windows on two sides and sets of French doors that open onto a verandah on the third side. These all afford abundant light and provide a cross-breeze that keeps the tiles cool even in the summer. In the night this coolness permeates the room.

The guest bedroom (see overleaf) takes the same advantage of tiled floors, but here, where the tiles are only simple white squares, they have been overlaid with a sisal area rug. Surrounding the bed, this is also more inviting for bare feet on winter mornings.

(Right) *A sketch from the 1950s of India's mother, Lady Pamela Hicks, stands on an easel.*

(Left) *Barrel, our island "potcake," (a mixed breed dog) contemplates life from a long Indian chaise.*

The guest room is painted white throughout and is flooded with sunlight in the early morning and the evening but shaded in the afternoon. Tropical bird prints and botanical prints show some signs of wear and tear but, again, this is a lived-in house.

(Left) *The armchair and headboard have been paint-stripped to match the paleness of the rest of the room.*

(Overleaf) *A bedside table holds a pre-war photograph of India's grandmother, Lady Edwina Mountbatten, along with sketchbooks and journals that await any inspiration guests or family might have.*

The walls came down

The kitchen had been designed for the days when it was the exclusive province of staff. It was made up of four distinct and small areas: a pantry, a larder, preparation space, and the kitchen itself.

In a house filling up with a growing, young family, such kitchens have become a thing of the past. These days a family

needs to be able not only to sit and chat in the same room while meals are being prepared, but also, increasingly, to entertain there.

(Above and right) The kitchen is the only room in the house that needed renovation rather than redecorating to solve its problems.

(Above and opposite)
The shaded courtyard set up for lunch with shells and
flowers and rather exotic cocktail glasses in the shape
of palm trees, found in Miami.

The courtyard beyond the kitchen is partly covered, which works well for any meal of the day. The walls shelter it from wind, and the sitting area is equally sheltered from the rain and the direct sun in the heat of the day.

Half in and half out of the house, the courtyard is lined with flowerbeds and pots in which grow tropical fruit and flowers, including tangerines, bananas, and pineapples, along with birds of paradise and night-blooming jasmine. Purple bougainvillea crowds over the courtyard wall.

The house on
the hill

A movable feast

One of the pleasures to be taken advantage of by living in a warm climate is eating outside. Breakfast, lunches, dinners, and occasionally teatimes are set up in the garden or courtyard or even on the brow of a hill, because diversifying the location of meals adds greatly to the pleasure.

Table settings change constantly, too. The china may be intermixed from collection to collection, lending a "mad hatter's tea party" feel, but usually a calmer, more sophisticated look takes over with only one set of white china.

Breakfasts tend to have an arrangement of fruit laid out but flowers are always added to the table later in the day. Smaller, more timid bunches of varied colours in tiny vases are placed in front of each setting for a lunch party, or grander, taller arrangements of neutral colour for a dinner. Both breakfast and lunch find the tables covered in a white linen cloth, especially as these tend to be the hotter times to be eating. Occasionally at a dinner party we will be more adventurous and cover the table in

The idea of setting formal tables out in the open came from travelling on safari in Africa. While we don't have to keep an eye out for buffalo, lion, or hippo here, there are some wild animals of our own to contend with.

an Indian bedspread, navy blue with tiny mirrors sewn all over it, or multi-patterned in pale pinks and rust reds.

The decorations change, too – bleached sand dollars are scattered across the table top, or pastel pink conch shells are collected together in the centre as a kind of sculpture. Starfish may also grace the table from time to time, often hand-painted to match a setting.

Teatimes are quite infrequent, but if the effort has been made, then a game of croquet or canasta will definitely follow.

In the evening, when the warmth of the day is wearing off, we will light torches around the table and have two huge silver candelabra burning. If we happen to be eating in the courtyard, then we may light lanterns and hang them in the branches of the hibiscus bushes.

Once in a full moon we eat on the beach, with a long rustic wooden picnic table set up with benches running down either side. Few candles are needed on a night like this as the moon is generous with her light.

*(Above) We have the great good luck to have a friend on the island
who grows roses. Appropriately, she is called Rosie and also happens
to be one of the best airplane pilots in these islands.*

*(Right) The dining room, laid out in the early evening for a
formal dinner.*

Our dining room is relatively formal and nowadays probably the location least used for entertaining. In the wintertime, or when the weather is too rough, we use it – but with the light from its rather over-the-top chandelier, the table is more often used for late-night card games.

Rain or shine, whether we are entertaining inside or outside we take a lot of time and trouble to "art direct" the scene that greets guests. This may be a product of upbringing or of living on a tiny island with no horizons (leading to excessive attention to small details); or it may simply be the result of not having full-time jobs. But taking the sort of trouble normally associated with film sets, to create temporary "tablescapes," often makes us both late for our own parties.

As silly as all this effort may seem, it is not purely "showing off," as guests should have a feast for the eyes and indeed for all of the senses when they sit at the table.

*(Overleaf) The jaw of a tiger shark – brought back from Africa –
which often stands in the dining room to inspire a good appetite. Here,
the jaw's scale is well demonstrated.*

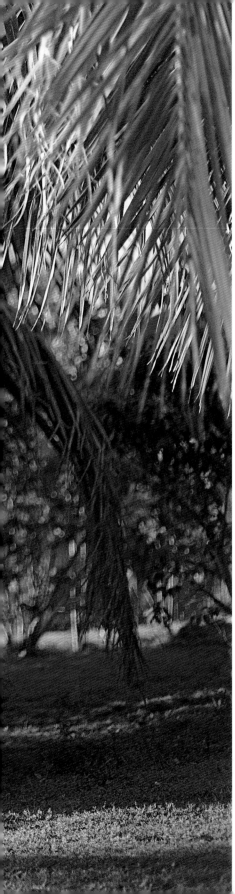

An outpost of empire

The plantation feel of Hibiscus Hill was seeping out of the woodwork and across the lawn when we designed this playhouse. With jalousie shutters on three of the six sides and a stable door (Dutch door), it has a cedar shingle roof. Inside we stained the wood floor dark and hung framed black-and-white photographs on the walls.

It was important to keep the playhouse in the same style as everything around even though it had been built for the children. This rule applies throughout the property – the children's bedrooms and schoolroom were also designed to be colonial in feel. Old-fashioned wooden toys help to achieve this.

Like a lot of first-time parents, we tried to have no plastic toys. Now it's not even a guideline, let alone a rule.

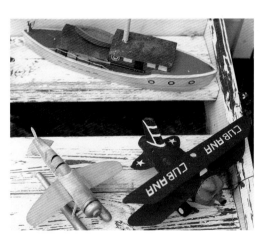

The playhouse looks like some outpost from the North-West Frontier. The scene of terrific pitched battles, it also comes under the civilizing influence of visiting girl cousins, becoming the setting for scenic tea parties.

Climbing for Coconuts in the Bahamas Colour by Larry Witt

A 1960s postcard.

We still have our tallest coconut palms trimmed before the hurricane season. Soon
we won't have to pay anyone to do it, as the boys practise before bedtime.

Apart from the boys, the other wild things growing in the garden are the plants and trees, which are also slowly coming under control.

Over the past five years we have done a lot of work on the garden, which had been rather neglected. Most of the effort has gone into getting some order and shape into things but it is by no means formal.

We have in fact decided to remove almost all colour – the only remaining flowers are bougainvillea and oleander. All the plants are tropical and the garden is every shade of green imaginable, a sort of semi-tamed jungle.

We have around two hundred coconut palms along with areca, Alexander, fishtail, Chinese fan, Christmas (so called for their red berries), and traveller's palms.

Scaevola, pandanus, acacia, Spanish bayonets (yucca), schefflera, and ficus act as hedges and barriers. Big trees include a poor-man's-orchid and tabebuia, along with a bank of royal poinciana that flower with such violent, red blooms that it looks as if the town is on fire.

A bismarckia palm,
the flagship of the garden, shades a corner of the terrace
laid out ready for cocktails.

The great enemies of all this hard work are, of course, hurricanes. In the summertime we keep an eye on the weather constantly. Along with everything else that one has to lose, one of the most painful experiences is to come outside after "a blow" to see smashed and twisted plants with their leaves burnt off by the salt, and coconut palms lying uprooted on their sides. The price of living in this paradise, hurricanes are God's pruning. Encouragingly, anything that survives often comes back even stronger after the initial shock.

That probably goes for all of us.

Hibiscus Hill lit up at night.

When the house is quiet and the boys asleep, a walk to the end of the garden never

fails to remind us of our good luck.

Plantation style

Building a house overlooking the ocean for our family and guests.

A house for the guests

The Guest House is set in a grove of palm trees behind Hibiscus Hill and on the crest of the dunes. Built in the "plantation style" to look as though it had always been there, it has an imposing staircase leading to the first of two large verandahs.

As a beach house in the tropics, it has to remain as cool as possible throughout the year. Following a tropical tradition, this was achieved by building the house on four pylons, which allow air to circulate around and under the house. It also helps protect the rooms from hurricane flooding.

The house was built to face south, a unique decision for this island, as all other homes look directly west or east, in order to avoid the strong midday sun as much as possible. The south-facing aspect gives guests a chance to sit, cocktail in hand, on the upper verandah as the sun sets, to watch the light changing over both the bay and the Atlantic. From up here you can hear the ever-present breeze in the casuarina trees, the rustling of the palms below, and the distant sound of a motor on the bay. A clear, stretching view of the pink sand beach beneath the property is another advantage of the top verandah. From this height one can spot a stray guest or an escaping child.

The sitting room and two master guest rooms are upstairs, leaving the dining room, kitchen, and remaining bedrooms downstairs. A hammock is slung between two trees at the bottom of the stairs so guests may stumble outside and into it, straight from a long lunch into a siesta.

Plantation
style

The Guest House, built in only nine months,
was completed seven weeks before a 165 mile-per-hour (280km-per-hour) hurricane hit
the island. The house is still there.

The inside is made entirely of wood. Everything was painted white, which gives it a simple, cool, and calm atmosphere intended to suit nearly everyone's taste. The deckchairs in the dining room lend a beach feel, tying in with the nautical lamps standing on a second-hand chest

of drawers. The chest was covered by hand, using old sailing maps and a lot of white (PVA) glue.

(*Above*) *Outsize hurricane*
lamps are half filled with layers of pink sand from the beach and black sand
from Capolbia, south of Rome.

(Opposite) *Maps of surrounding islands are held in frames made by the*
carpenters who worked on the house, and stained by us.

(Overleaf) *A second-hand chest, covered by us in nautical charts.*

WEST INDIES

ATLANTIC OCEAN

EAST

S.ta Mark
St Matheo
St John
St Augustin
Bay of Apalache
FLORIDA
Lake George
C Cannaveral
Savanna R
Joseph's Bay
St Second Lagoon
piritu Santo
Rock Point
Charlotte Haven
Carlos Bay
Spiritu Santo L.
Punta Large
GULF OF FLORIDA
The Promontory
C Florida
The Martyr's Reef
FLORIDA STREAM

BAHAMA OR
LUCAYOS
ISLANDSE.

Abaco
Lit. Bank of Bahama
Great Bahama
Lucayoneoue
the Hole in the Rock
Biminis
Providence
Alabaster &
Eleuthera
Providence Ch.
Espiritu
Santo or
GREAT
Andros I.
Cayo de Sal
Anguilla
BANK
OF BAHAMA
BAHAMA CHANNEL
Jardin del Rey
Guanahani or
S. Salvador
Warlands I.
Exuma
Stocking
Exuma Sound
Rum Key
Yuma or
Long I.
Verd I.
Atwoods Key
Crooked I
Mayaguana
Acklins Key
The Corcos or les Cayques
Long Key
Litt Inagua
Turks Is.
Handkercheif Shoal
A Shoal

HAVANAH
St Cruz
Cadiz
CUBA
Isabella
Batabana
la Trinidad
Jardin de la Reyna
OLD
Spirith Santo
del Rey
Villa del Principe
Nipe
B Mahon
Inagua
Tortugas
PASSAGE
St Salvador del Baymo
S.t Jago
St Nicholas
B of Samana
Samana I
Port Paix
Caye du Nord
le Cap Francois
pt Carouge
Old C Francois
S.t Jago el Coticy
Cape du Nord

CUBA OF
Little Cayman
Great Cayman
Pracel
Negril by North
Negril by South
JAMAICA E.
Spanish Town
Savanna la Mar
Pedro Bluff
Port Royal
Portland Pt
Pedro Shoals
Channel del Cruz
C de Cruz
Portillo
Torquino R.
Guana Sevilla
Pt de Berracos
Galina Pt Guantanamo
Kingston
C. WINDWARD
C. Dame Marie
Pt Irois
Pt Morant
la Gonoy
Petit Guaves
St Louis
Pt.d Abacon
Beata
C de la Beata

HISPANIOLA OR St DOMINGO
The Western part belongs to the French, the Eastern by the Spaniards ce-
-ded to the French in 1796.

Port au Prince
St Domingo
C del Engano
Saona
C. Roxo
THE VIRGIN ISLANDS
Anegada E.
C de St Juan
C de St Thomas Du
Tortola
Virgin Corda E.
St Johns Da
Anguilla E.
St Martins E.
St Bartholomew E.
St Eufatia
Berbuda E.
St Christophers E.
Antigua E.
PORTORICOS
St Juan
St Croix Da
Saba Du

HONDURAS

Serrenilla
The New Boar
The Bugles
Pedro Shoals

CARIBBEAN SEA

LEEWARD
ISLANDS
Aves I.
Mousserat E.
Deseada E.
Grand Terre E.
Guadaloupe E.
Basse-terre
Marie Galante E.
Charlotte Town
Dominica E.

Swan Islands
Carrantasea
Lag.
Brewers Lag.
Carrantasea Shoals
Seeklong
C Gracios a Dios
Para Lago
Guana Reef
Pearl Is.
Tangulaw
Old Providence
Mosquitos
Pearl Key
Little Corn I
Corn I.
St Andres
Great Corn I
Hone sound
Ramas
St Juans R.
Cuckeral
Bocataro
Provision I
Porto Bello
la Conception
Pt de St Blas
Sambaltas Is.
Costa Rica
VERAGUA
Panama
St Jago
DARIE
Gulf of
Morosquillo
Pt de Caribana
Gulf of Darien
Sinu
St Sebastian
Tamaimeque

THE SPANISH MAIN

Ft St Pierre
Martinico E.
F Royal
St Lucia E.
THE WINDWARD ISLANDS
Bridge Town
Kingstown
St Vincent
Fort Royal
Granada E.
Barbad
Tobago E.
Trinidad S.
St Joseph

THE GRANADINES

C de la Vela
Pt de Piedras
C de Chichibacoa
Orua Du
Curacao Du
Buen aire Du
Orchilla Is.
Blanca
Tortuga Salada
la Margarita S.
PARIA
GUARAUNOS

los Monges
Pt Honda
los Monges
Pueblo
C Roman
Aves I.
Chica I.
la Guayra
C Codora
G of Triste
Gof Carriaco
Carriaco
CARACAS
Cumana
CUMANA

R Grande de la Madalena
St Martha
Salamanca
Gulf of Venezuela
Ft Carlos
Maracaybo
SANTA MARTHA
Malambito
Teneriff
Momox
Merida
Gibraltar
CARTHAGENA
Carthagena or I de Varu
VENEZUELA
Lake of Maracaybo
Laguna
Luguna
Maracaybo
Carora
Corora
Valencia
Leon de Caracas
Baraquicimeto
Calabeza
TERRA FIRMA
Guayana
Tolu
Guayana
PARIA

Pride compels us to show off the outside and its setting once more.

Plantation
style

A taste of the tropics

Living on the island means an abundance of fruit, and we take full advantage of this, using it as decoration throughout the house. Often the entrance hall greets guests with a dish laden with pineapples, the Caribbean sign of friendship and welcome. Our drinks tray will have a basket of lemons and limes nestling beside it, and

a salad bowl of mangoes or papayas sits on the kitchen table. Occasionally we will fill an open fireplace with bowls of fruit, and whenever available, a bunch or branch of baby bananas hangs on the open terrace.

Plantation
style

Simple symmetry

Whereas Hibiscus Hill, in true Bahamian form, has a mass of higgledy-piggledy rooms, which have been added one by one as the family has grown over the years, the Guest House offered the chance to go for a more symmetrical theme. Thus the reception rooms and the kitchen run from front to back and fill the centre, flanked on both sides by bedrooms and bathrooms on both floors. This modular floor plan also means that there is no wasted space, and with all the doors and windows open the cross-ventilation is excellent. The style of the house is as simple as the floor plan – everything is either painted white or stained a dark shade.

The sitting room is white, with dark mahogany-stained floors. It is dominated by a large coffee table that we designed, and two sofas. Above these hang two collections of photographs. The majority of the frames are dark wood to echo the dark floor.

There are no blinds or curtains in the sitting room. The joy of living or staying in this part of the world is to see the light and altering heavens as much as possible, in particular the clear, brilliant night skies.

Plantation style

Although there is overhead lighting, every side table has its own lamp, which gives a gentle and more compassionate light.

The large table is used to display an ever-changing group of photographic books and wooden games such as backgammon and solitaire, along with bowls and baskets of shells from the local beaches. The large, bleached conch shells also double as very effective doorsteps on windy days.

As with our other projects, we have tried to incorporate some rattan into the Guest House. Just in front of the coffee table are two large rattan plantation chairs. In our experience these chairs speak for themselves, denoting a sense of style and time.

As in our own home, a large spray of palm fronds lends colour to the room, and is particularly effective here as the French doors look out over the tops of the coconut trees.

*The "tray ceilings" throughout the upper floor
are traditional in the islands. They add height to the room
and help the fans to circulate air. The four French doors (two
act as sidelights) give a panoramic view at treetop height,
southwards and over the ocean. The rattan planter's chairs are
a simple shorthand motif for a sense of the tropics, and, by
their very name, hark back to an age
of plantations.*

The walls above the sofas are hung with a gallery of black-and-white and sepia photographs. Some are of Nassau from the 1930s and '40s. Some were given to India by the Maharaja of Jodhpur, when we were staying at his palace in Rajasthan, and show her grandfather playing polo. One picture is simply a stolen menu cover from a restaurant in New York called Indochine. The remaining photographs were taken by us.

Most of this collection hangs in dark
wood or black frames, surrounded with
cream or white mounts (mats). The use
of only two colours of frames and
mounts pulls together this disparate
group. The birdcage is an easy and
effective ornament, and is sturdy
enough to withstand the small and
inquisitive hands of visiting children.
It adds to the overall plantation feel
that this house exudes.

"Scrap wall"

Filling scrapbooks just wasn't enough. This wall is an ever-shifting exhibition, which was easy to put together by tacking odd bits and pieces into the wood. Continuing the ubiquitous island theme, the dark wood printer's tray has been lovingly filled with shells, collected, cleaned, and compartmentalized, from deep-sea diving around the islands.

Other accessories and furniture also lend a personal touch to this corner of the house. The painting of the house above the printer's tray is a cherished present. A writer's lamp stands significantly on a writer's desk, with more island treasures dotted about on top. The chair has a twin, hidden inside a bedroom. Both were inherited with the main house – they were a shocking shade of blue when we found them. A liberal use of elbow grease and sandpaper produced surfaces we could paint white, and then we covered the seats and back in a subtle pineapple fabric.

A three-dimensional collage, situated over a writing desk, was created using paintings, envelopes, photographs, CD covers, postcards, and cuttings from magazines as well as a printer's hot-metal type tray, which is filled with shells found by India while diving.

KOOKABURRA SPEEDBOAT
Sydney Harbour

(Above) A model sailboat on top of a chest of drawers in a bedroom.

(Opposite) Sepia-toned photographs of classic yachts taken by David in the South of France.

Sail away

Having researched "plantation style" quite well, we thought it best to follow the simple rules that the term imposes, while adding our own small touches of drama. For example, in the bedroom of the Guest House, an uncomplicated white chest of drawers, framed by the tongue-and-groove wall, has a model sailboat placed on top of it.

An armchair placed beneath a set of photographs was visualized in the same vein. A straw hat, casually tossed onto the chair, contrasts dramatically with the geometrically hung sepia photographs.

Bed making

The "pencil beds", so-called because of their tall, tapering posts, were devised by us, specifically with guests in mind. The design needed to be simple and elegant, in keeping with the house, and yet one that most friends would feel comfortable in.

While the mosquito netting is solely for cosmetic purposes and serves only really to create atmosphere, it also allows the breeze to blow through.

(Right and opposite) The "pencil beds," which we also designed, were hand-made by the carpenters. We wanted each of the beds to be draped in a similar fashion, with a moustiquaire. As the mosquito netting for the beds wasn't available locally, we bought a hundred yards (90m) of it in Goa and carried it back. It was cheap but heavy.

Following the plantation theme, we used bolsters behind the pillows, to give the beds the requisite old-fashioned feel.

If we had dared, we would have lit all the rooms with candles, but, sadly, the lighting is of the electric kind, so bedside lamps adorn each bedside table.

Once again we chose not to hang any curtains or blinds – instead, the bedrooms are shuttered. In the daytime, with these half-closed, a wonderful shadow spills out across the room.

Out in the open

Everyone spends a moment or even a day on one of the verandahs — they really are the focal point of the Guest House. With this in mind we designed an extra-wide space to incorporate furniture. The sofa, armchair, and cushions have all been fashioned from modern materials that can be left outside all year round. Thankfully,

The verandahs of the Guest House catch the summer trade winds and are sheltered in the winter. About forty feet (12m) long and twelve feet (3.5m) wide, they give views of the Sargasso Sea to the east and the bay on the Caribbean side.

Plantation
style

these materials, despite being plastic-based, look a good deal like rattan. The little wooden boat and native conch shell are often used as doorstops. As always, we chose with care colours that were sympathetic to our interiors: cream-coloured cushions and beige chairs and sofas.

Vestiges of grandeur

The chance to restore a plantation house inn after the destruction caused by a massive hurricane.

A brass telescope keeps watch over the approach to the harbour from the attic of The Landing Hotel.

Making the old work with the new

One of the most architecturally significant buildings on the island, The Landing Hotel is the first sight of the town for visitors as they arrive on the Government Dock (hence the hotel's name).

The main house, built as the home of a sugar plantation owner in 1800, is now linked by a garden with "The Captain's House," built for a seafarer in 1820. The main house forms a perfect square and the wide, wraparound verandahs are shaded from the afternoon sun by the steep, pitched roof. Both the roof and the verandah were largely torn off by Hurricane Floyd in 1999, filling the rooms with a foot (30cm) of rain water.

The owners, who are half Bahamian and half Australian, were already good friends of ours. With the buildings and the business potentially ruined, we initially suggested we get involved in the redesign and the decoration of just the bedrooms. However, we soon realized that there was little point in doing half the job, so we invested our own money to become partners and set about a restoration of the entire property.

We had the experience of building and decorating our own version of a plantation house, and a previous trip around some of the woefully over-renovated historic houses and inns of Mississippi had convinced us that we wanted to create a "lived-in" house from the 1800s.

Vestiges of
grandeur

(Opposite) *A white Adirondack chair*
on a verandah outside one of the bedrooms. The white decks, louvred partitions, and furniture, help to bounce light into the rooms.

(Previous page) *The Landing Hotel. The two buildings are perfect examples of colonial architecture and were*
constructed in 1800 and 1820.

Budget was a key consideration (as it tends to be when you are spending your own money). Timing was the other important factor, because of the need to get the hotel business back up and running as quickly as possible.

In terms of both time and money, it is extraordinary how much can be achieved when everyone pitches in, both in designing and in the physical tasks of restoration – particularly when a degree of imperfection is preferable to making the finished project look as though it had been built yesterday.

(Left and right)

These mint green Adirondack chairs sit on dark-stained verandahs. Their tilted-back design works particularly well because of the steep angle of the deck, which is designed to help the run-off of rain water.

The wide verandahs were restored and set out with Adirondack chairs that were found on the island. Set back in the shade, they convey a "planter's club" feel to the verandah, overlooking the comings and goings of the harbour. This is the best place to sit with coffee or a cocktail and watch the unloading of the mail boat from Nassau.

Setting the clock back

After replacing the cedar shingle roof and the verandahs, attention was turned to the inside of the buildings. We were able to keep most of the original wooden floors and the main walls, which are almost two feet (60cm) thick and made of stone. Apart from these structural "bones," it was pretty much a case of starting from scratch.

Prior to the hurricane in 1999, The Landing had hardly been decorated since the 1970s. Even then, the changes had been fairly unsympathetic to the character of the buildings. For instance, the passageway between the dining room and bar had a partition wall with a small doorway – in the dark gloom beyond, a couple of chests of drawers containing silverware and table linen supported a coffee machine and cash register.

Simply removing the partition opened up the flow of light and traffic, and what had been a corridor became a coffee and cigar counter (exploiting one of the privileges of living two hours from Havana).

We set about designing a counter and storage space that could be made quickly and relatively inexpensively. Made from plywood and crown moulding, it consisted of a series of "pigeonholes" constructed like hinged picture frames with glass panels. The design was based on an apothecary's shop in Havana's Old Town. It took two long nights to stain the whole thing to look like mahogany.

While we produced detailed drawings with measurements, our designs were allowed to work thanks to the skill of the local carpenter who had built the Guest House. After two hundred years, few or none of the floors are level and almost none of the corners form true right angles, so each piece had to be made to measure.

The details on the fascia of the counter were achieved by attaching halved balustrades.

The cigar and coffee counter made from plywood and picture glass and then stained to appear mahogany. Our drawings were brought to life by Scott Lewis, a young local carpenter.

It is so easy to decorate using natural elements from the beach. Here, a straw dish is piled high with bleached coral ...

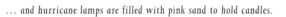

... and hurricane lamps are filled with pink sand to hold candles.

Serious business

We based the redesign of the bar on the picture that is created in the mind's eye by Ernest Hemingway and Graham Greene novels. The significance of the "cocktail hour" has not diminished despite the passing of colonial times.

The design of a bar is a particularly interesting challenge. It needs to be decorative in order to create an atmosphere that will draw business, and it must be functional so that a bartender can find, reach, and dispense quickly when busy.

Decoratively, the fun comes from the display of bottles and their exotic labels, with the implied adventure that their combinations carry. The same often goes for the other side of the bar, where a mixture of ferry-men and fisher-men rub shoulders with crowned heads, super-models, and film actors.

The bar, where the alchemy of mixing drinks is often as
exotic as the mixture of people drinking them.

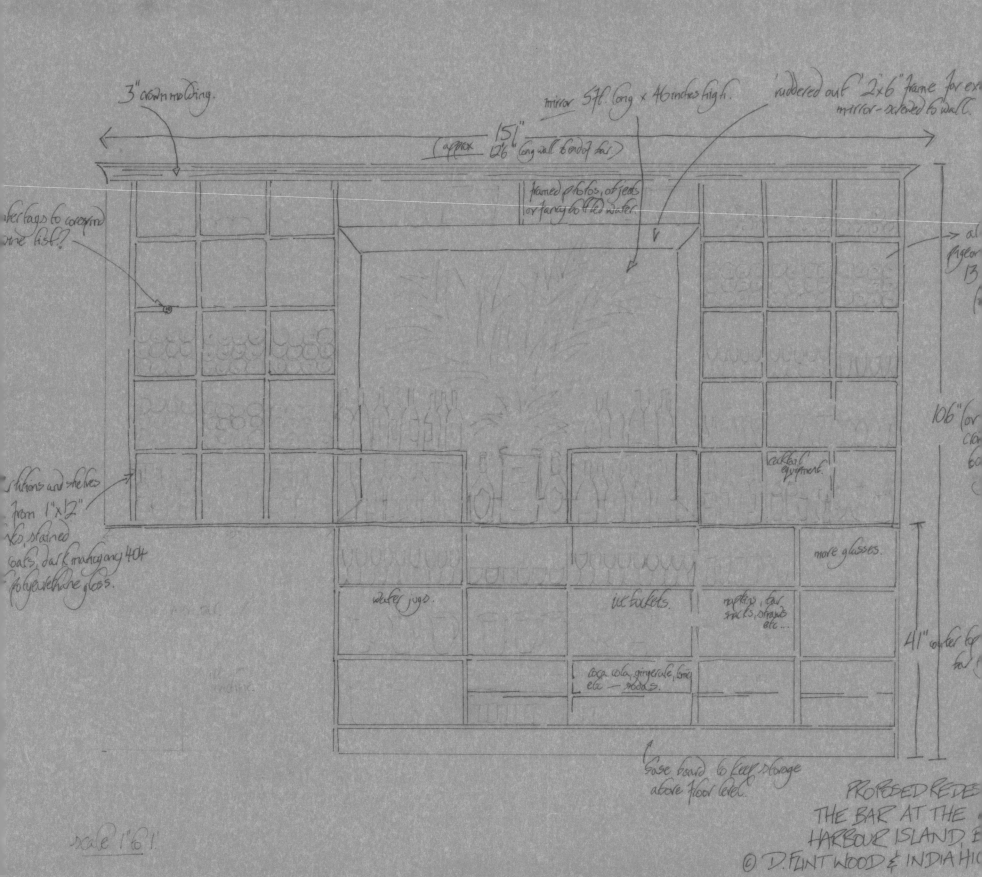

3" crown molding.

mirror 5ft. long × 46 inches high.

'ruddered out' 2"×6" frame for ex
mirror - screwed to wall.

approx 151"
126" (long wall to end of bar.)

framed photos, of jeds
or fancy bottled water.

...ber tags to correspond
wine list.?

al...
pigeon
13

106" (or
clo...
60

...litions and shelves
from 1"×12"
...s, stained
coats, dark mahogany 404
polyurethane gloss.

cocktail
equipment.

more glasses.

water jugs.

ice buckets.

napkins, bar
snacks, straws
etc...

41" counter for
bar t...

coca cola, ginger ale, tonic
etc — sodas.

base board to keep storage
above floor level.

scale 1"6'1

PROPOSED REDE...
THE BAR AT THE
HARBOUR ISLAND, B...
© D. FLINT WOOD & INDIA HIC...

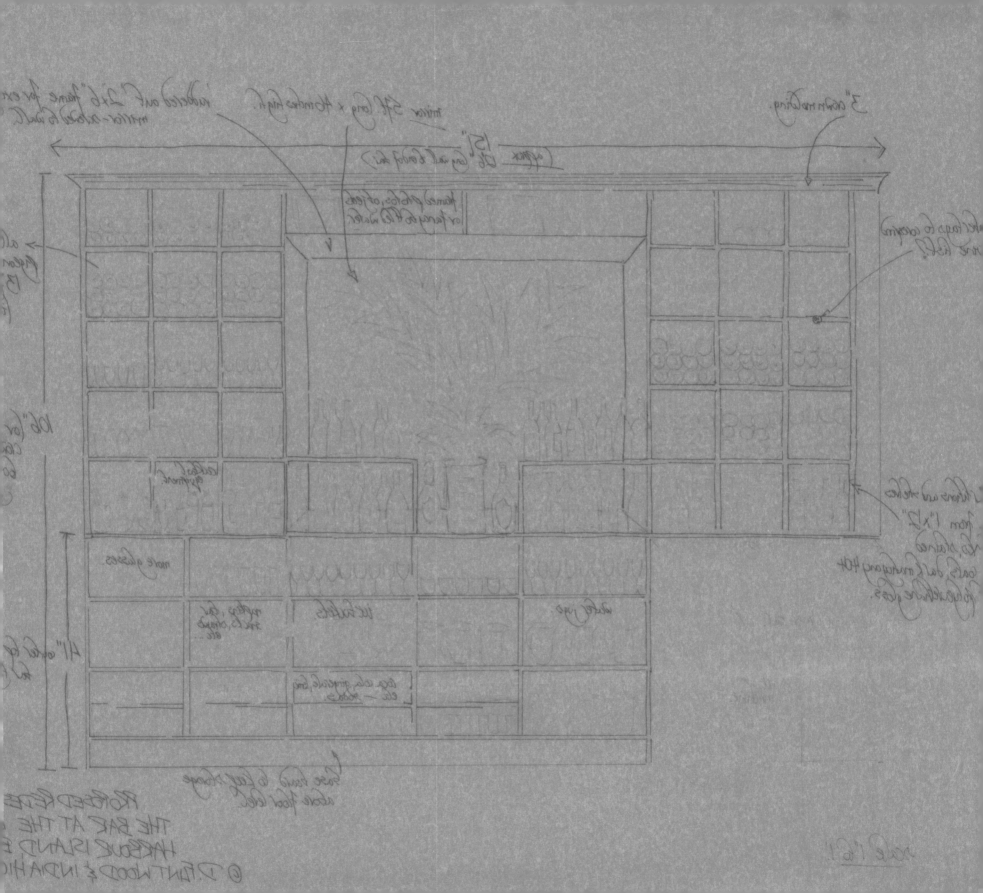

Family business

In keeping with The Landing's origins as a plantation house, every effort was made to retain the sense of a private home, rather than an institutional hotel. All of the rooms, including the public ones, contain personal details serving as reminders that this is a family-run business and that the family has its roots in these islands.

Brenda Barry, one of the hotel's owners, was the first Miss Bahamas, in 1961. She has a wonderful archive of her modelling days and family photographs that are framed and hung, like a gallery, in the sitting area of the bar. The only problem she encountered was having to edit them.

Although all the other rooms are painted white, the dining room and the bar are a butter yellow, which is a soft and inviting colour when lit at night. In the corners of the bar are four-, five-, and six-pointed starfish, backlit by tea lights. As on the preceding pages, it is simple and effective to use coral, shells, and sand for decorative details.

The seating area of the bar, where planter's chairs and sofas are crowned by family photographs. The seemingly random pattern of photographs and the diverse frames allow the eye to wander without emphasizing any particular picture.

(Overleaf) The bar was designed to look like it came from a Hemingway novel, and was made from the simplest of materials: plywood and maghogany stain.

Just as shells, coral, and sand are used to decorate, so tropical fruit lends itself

to simple but dramatic "still lifes."

The advantage of these "still lifes" is that they become active ingredients in rum punches

and daiquiris — nothing goes to waste.

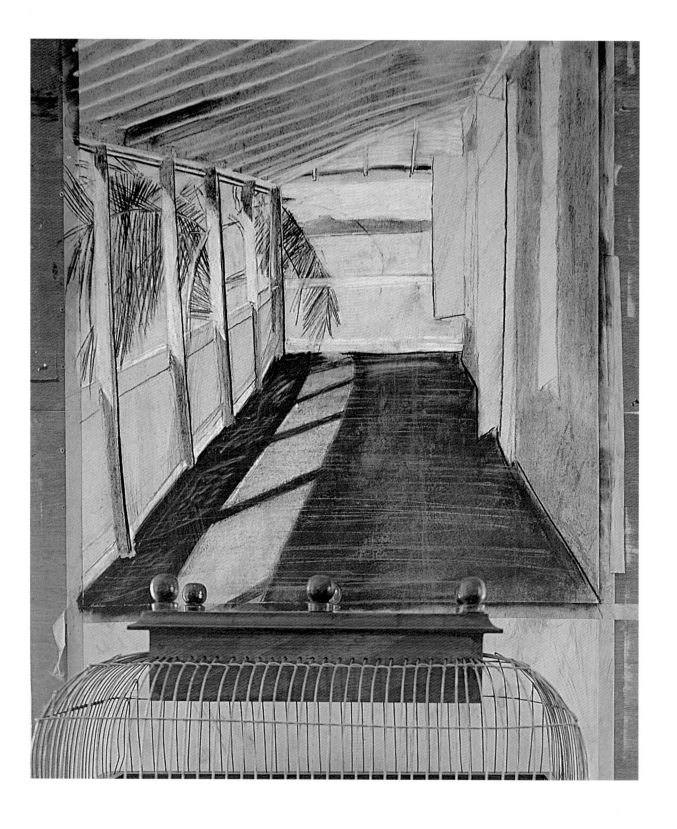

Made in the shade

Much of island life is spent out of doors, particularly for visitors. But if you have had enough of the sun or if the weather worsens, it is a relief to have somewhere to sit quietly.

The large room upstairs in the main house became a library and sitting room for just this purpose. It is also sometimes used as a private dining room, separate from the restaurant downstairs.

In any of these roles, it is designed to reinforce the atmosphere of the original plantation house or perhaps, now that it is a public space, to have the feeling of a private club.

The room has windows and a glass door on two sides that open onto the main verandah, which overlooks the harbour to the west and Bay Street to the north. You can sit here and mind your own business or just about everybody else's.

The substantial door and window frames were stripped of their centuries of paint layers without being cleaned up too much. Elements of past filler and streaks of ingrained paint were simply left. Finally, two coats of stain varnish were applied to achieve a look somewhere between conventional liming (pickling) and just plain "beaten up."

(Opposite) This sketch of the verandah was found in the basement cellar, stuck with masking tape to a sheet of plywood.

(Right) If you step through the doorway that the sketch hangs beside, you see the artist's original view.

Less is more

To some extent a fairly minimal room, the library possibly comes as close as any to the look and feel that such a space may have had in a house of its period. Despite its lack of clutter and its apparent formality, it is an extremely comfortable room to spend time in.

The greatest assets, in terms of both appearance and comfort, are the large sofa and giant armchair made of wood and rattan by Ralph Lauren. We had a great deal of help acquiring them from the company just as they were being launched as part of a new line.

Although furniture like this is naturally expensive, spending on one or two "signature" pieces for a room, rather than filling it with nondescript things, has far more impact. More often than not, such a piece also lasts longer and is more comfortable.

The portraits, but not the frames, that hang above the sofa were "borrowed" from the Hicks family home in England. Unfortunately, David Hicks would not release the original oval, gilt frames. Since we could not get new frames made in London, New York or Miami for less than a small fortune, we had the frames cut out of plywood and then stained them ourselves.

The embodiment of plantation style — a rattan sofa sits beneath
a pair of eighteenth-century portraits.

The simple yet impressive library bookcases were designed by us for this room. Made by a local carpenter, they were constructed inside the room. Once again, the furniture was stained a dark mahogany in keeping with the "plantation" feel. The books themselves may not be as organized as we would wish, but with a multitude of guests passing through, there was little control. They were originally placed according to colour and height to give some kind of classified effect and, at the same time, pleasure to the eye. Filling the spaces between books is a collection of eccentricities, photograph frames, beauty pageant trophies, shells, and so on.

Hidden away inside one of the matching bookcases is a television, which is generally only used during very bad weather.

Tropical flowers picked from the hotel's garden are placed daily in the library and also in the bedrooms.

Through the French doors are two plantation chairs luxuriously waiting for a new guest, and between them a standing lamp. Here, as in most of the hotel, the lighting is from lamps and never overhead.

Vestiges of grandeur

Until the library was refurbished, nearly all of our designs for cabinetry had been built-in. The bookcases in the library, however, were designed as standing pieces with fairly ornate mouldings at the top. They were made on site.

"In the afternoon…"

If the inspiration for the bar and the cigar counters is from literature like *Our Man in Havana* and *Islands in the Stream*, then our clues for the bedrooms came more directly from films like *Casablanca*, *The English Patient*, and *Sheltering Sky*.

The bedrooms are meant to live up to lines from Alfred Lord Tennyson's poem "The Lotus Eaters":

"In the afternoon they came unto a land in which it seemed always afternoon."

All of the rooms open out onto verandahs or terraces, and you could virtually lean out of some of the rooms to pluck papaya or breadfruit from trees in the garden.

The windows are hung with plantation shutters, which, in cinematic fashion, filter the sunlight into strips across the Indian mosquito netting and the old wooden floors.

Mirrors are an important element in each of the hotel bedrooms as they are used to bounce light around the room and enhance the feeling of spaciousness.

Vestiges of grandeur

A large framed mirror above the writing desk reflects
an English hand-coloured seashell print from 1790.
Hopefully the desk and the overall atmosphere inspire
suitably evocative letters and postcards home from
the tropics.

Vestiges of
grandeur

Vestiges of
grandeur

Facing the office, where hotel clients check in, this concierge holding a guest book was drawn by India.

Vestiges of
grandeur

As in the Guest House, pine panelled doors were stained to match the rest of the dark wood, and given antiqued brass door handles. Each room is named after a tropical flower and the name was hand-painted by us in brass paint with black shadowing on each door.

The floors are made of Abaco pine, native to the Caribbean. Probably laid in 1800 when the house was built, they are now worn smooth by two hundred years of traffic and weather.

For the beds, we repeated the theme of the "pencil beds" that we had designed originally for our Guest House. Relatively inexpensive desks and side tables made in Indonesia were bought to complement them.

The art in every room varies, ranging from oil paintings and antique prints to sand dollars and white seashells mounted in wooden partitioned box frames.

(Left) A partitioned box frame displaying white shells from the beach.

(Opposite) Seen from the bed, a rattan chaise longue sits in the breeze from a window overlooking the bay.

Under the eaves

The entire top floor of The Landing's second building, The Captain's House, is taken up by an attic dedicated to romance. As a diversion from the dark floors and furniture in the rest of the hotel, the attic is dominated by white.

Two large rooms that are to all intents and purposes mirror images of each other are separated by a central corridor. At the end of the corridor, in a shaft of sunlight from one of the dormer windows that project from the roof on all sides, sits a rather eccentric, Victorian chair. It was bought in a New York flea market and then re-covered in very pale grey.

To the right is the bathroom. The grey painted floor surrounds a white wooden dais, on which a large bathtub has been "dropped" into a panelled, white painted, wooden frame.

It seemed slightly humorous to have a bathroom as large as the bedroom, so we let the bath take the lead, even banishing the washbasin to a tiny cupboard.

On the basis that there is no greater decadence than chatting to someone while taking a bath, the room has two white, wicker-backed armchairs and a footstool. These were re-covered using a pink and white toile de Jouy fabric from what had been a bedcover.

The bedroom, across the corridor, reflects the same layout but with a gilt bed occupying the centre of the room. Bought in New Orleans, it is French and was made around 1890.

Blood-red hibiscus in white pottery sits on a bedside table.

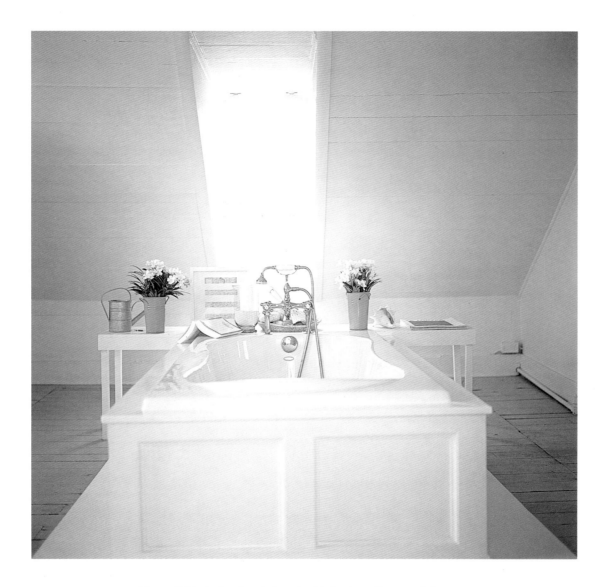

The panelled bathtub on its raised wooden dais dominates the centre of the room.

In the bedroom a Victorian gilt bed mirrors the layout of the bathroom next door.

(Overleaf) Flea market discoveries re-covered and placed for maximum dramatic impact
at the foot of the bath and in the corridor.

The last unrestored element at The Landing, an old Bahamian skiff sits in the garden, shaded by a breadfruit tree.

Vestiges of
grandeur

Savannah – a retreat

Reaching back towards the dawn of architecture for his inspiration, David Hicks brought an essence of the Nile Valley to this family residence.

Savannah restored

The ambitious restoration of Savannah, a beach house designed by David Hicks in the late 1960s, was finally undertaken after another hurricane roared through the Caribbean, severely damaging the roof and many of its furnishings. In deciding the extent of the restoration, the family considered not only their personal attachment to the house but also the respect due to it as a landmark.

Savannah will always stand out. Unlike any other house in this part of the world in design, it was conceived a few years after David Hicks returned from a trip to Egypt, having been inspired by the temple of King Zoser. Initially it provoked great alarm and astonishment, but this later turned to universal admiration.

The house was designed with a flat roof, an unusual choice in a country with a rainy season, but it lasted for over thirty years before it needed replacing. A new roof was constructed and coated with a rubber membrane, and all the outside walls were bleached to remove the build-up of mildew.

The long weathered deck surrounding the house was replaced and new sunbeds were brought in from the United States. Stripped of their cushions, they make interesting horizontal patterns against the vertical boards of the deck.

This house is such a contrast to either our home, hotel, or Guest House that it became a kind of colour therapy, even down to the bright beach towels.

Savannah –
a retreat

Savannah's sitting room remains today a mix of David Hicks's brilliance and our attempt to emulate it. All the doors and windows in the house still run from floor to ceiling, giving the house a light and airy feeling. The Perspex (Plexiglas) cube tables in white and yellow are as modern today as they were thirty years ago.

The fireplace now houses a collection of fishing buoys that have been washed up onto the Atlantic beach below the house; one or two are actually children's balls. Sometimes the buoys are put outside in the garden as a kind of moving sculpture, in which case fruit in bowls replaces them, but a fire is seldom lit.

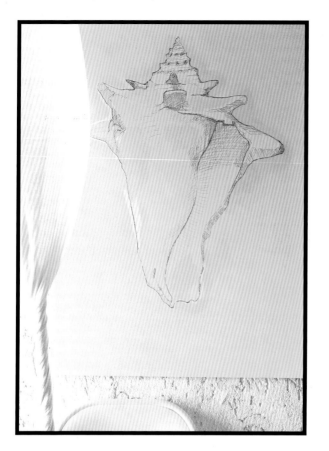

(Left) *The cement truck driving its way across the vast sisal rug is a reminder that even the interior walls throughout the house were roughly plastered with a mix of pink sand brought up from the beach.*

(Far left and above) *Doing jigsaws and drawings are the main holiday pursuits on this deserted island.*

The large, high-ceilinged sitting room is soft and cool, with bold sculptural paintings dominating it. The internal walls throughout are finished exactly as the external walls, in rough cement heavily mixed with the pinkish sand of the island.

Savannah –
a retreat

Caribbean colour schemes abound here, and there is no better example of this than the two paintings dominating either end of the sitting room.

Apart from these commissions all the artwork is by David Hicks, including a portrait of the 1960s model Twiggy, an ink sketch of his home in Oxfordshire, and geometric design experiments done on brown paper. These all hang on the walls today. The glue splotches on the brown paper designs now show through, all these years later, adding a little geometry of their own.

Two large scroll-top pictures were painted by
Bruce Tibbett especially for the house, and were commissioned
by David Hicks when it was constructed. Hung in the sitting
room, they anchor the two opposite seating areas. The Perspex
(Plexiglas) cube tables have not been moved for thirty-five
years, except when the new rug was laid down.

It was decided that the original architectural plan would remain intact. The only significant departure from the earlier design was a reconceived kitchen. We are not sure whether David Hicks ever chanced to go into the first one. There now stands a much roomier kitchen with all the necessary updates.

Colour is the main artery running through the house, clearly seen in the sculptures, paintings, furniture, and fabrics. Even the cement walls are a pastel shade of pink. The ceilings, however, create a sharp contrast, as they are smooth and white and have a narrow black painted gap all around to look as though they are floating. This idea was cleverly re-created in the bathrooms, which were designed simply using white Formica, and where the ceilings were done with the same effect. The washbasins, held up by brackets invisible to the eye, also "floated" out from the walls.

The lighting was dramatically theatrical in all of the rooms. Vast overhead spotlights shone down at certain points, illuminating a picture, a bed, or an antler head sculpture, but reading a book was nearly impossible. We have since ruined the effect by adding small modern side table spotlights that can be manoeuvred into position to make reading more comfortable.

The fact that this Egyptian fantasy was first photographed for an interiors magazine in 1973 and then again in 2003 for the same magazine is a testament to an extraordinary house and to a remarkable designer.

(Above) The dish mops were a brilliant touch suggesting a very tongue-in-cheek palm tree sculpture. This is also as old as the house. The kitten is new.

(Opposite) This sculpture is a child's interlocking toy.

Savannah —
a retreat

The dining room, as with most of the house, was kept to the original architectural plan. When the house
was completed in the 1960s, most of the furniture was shipped from England. This time around, most of it was purchased
over the Internet. On the far wall of the dining room is a collection of balustrades that David Hicks retrieved from derelict
homes or uninhabited shacks while trawling neighbouring settlements.

The bunk beds were built inside this bedroom. The polka dot bedspreads contrast with

the beds' rectilinear design.

Acknowledgements and Contacts

The authors would like to acknowledge, first and foremost Tracy and Brenda Barry and Toby Tyler for their friendship and partnership at The Landing (and particularly for the gracious way in which they accept our money, time and opinions!)

We would also like to thank all those who have helped us in our efforts both to make a home and family life here: Suzie Hickey, Tonton Orelus, Annette Hanna, Angela Stewart and above all Marissa Winder.

We thank Melissa Sellars and Tracy Barry for providing the ABC's and Hamish Bowles for the palm frond idea. We especially thank Pierre and Max for our transit camp.

We would also like to acknowledge all those individuals who helped make this book possible. Kate Oldfield and Claire Wedderburn-Maxwell, who guided this book through to completion. David Loftus for his creative talent and efforts against all odds, and Michel Arnaud for his collaboration. Paul Welti for his art direction and in understanding exactly what we thought we were trying to do.

To all those who helped on our projects, in particular the late Joe Barr, our friend Scott Lewis, Owen Higgs, Raymond Mather and William Higgs of Harbour Island, Franklyn Johnson, Don Johnson, Mekal Macdonald, Gordon Cash, "Gully" of Lower Bogue, North Eleuthera and Mr Leroy for his gardening enthusiasm.

To everybody else who has made us welcome, we never forget that we are strangers in a strange land.

The Guest House at Hibiscus Hill
A plantation-style house with four bedrooms and bathrooms along with forty-foot verandahs, surrounded by coconut trees on a hill overlooking the pink sand beach of Harbour Island in the Bahamas. The house is occasionally available to rent.
www.hibiscushillharbourisland.com
Fax: 001 242 333 2606

The Landing Hotel and Restaurant
A plantation house in the historic Dunmore Town on Harbour Island overlooking the harbour bay. With seven bedrooms and a restaurant, The Landing has won travel awards from *Condé Nast Traveller* and *Harpers and Queen*.
www.harbourislandlanding.com
Telephone: 001 242 333 2707

Savannah on Windermere Island
David Hicks' extraordinary holiday home, designed and built by him in 1969 and completely restored in 2002. It has four bedrooms and bathrooms and spectacular living spaces on this private island of Windermere in the Bahamas.
www.savannahwindermereisland.com
Fax: 001 242 333 2606